# DINOSAUR FACT DIG

# TRICERATOPS
## AND OTHER HORNED DINOSAURS
### THE NEED-TO-KNOW FACTS

BY
KATHRYN CLAY

Consultant: Mathew J. Wedel, PhD
Associate Professor
Western University of Health Services

raintree
a Capstone company — publishers for children

Raintree is an imprint of Capstone Global Library Limited, a company incorporated in England and Wales having its registered office at 264 Banbury Road, Oxford, OX2 7DY – Registered company number: 6695582

**www.raintree.co.uk**
myorders@raintree.co.uk
Text © Capstone Global Library Limited 2016
The moral rights of the proprietor have been asserted.

Edited by Michelle Hasselius
Designed by Kristi Carlson
Picture research by Wanda Winch
Production by Gene Bentdahl

ISBN 978 1 474 71940 7 (hardcover)
20 19 18 17 16
10 9 8 7 6 5 4 3 2 1

ISBN 978 1 474 71953 7 (paperback)
21 20 19 18 17
10 9 8 7 6 5 4 3 2 1

**British Library Cataloguing in Publication Data**
A full catalogue record for this book is available from the British Library.

**ACKNOWLEDGEMENTS**
All images by Jon Hughes except: MapArt (maps), Shuttershock: Elena Elisseeva, green gingko leaf, Jiang Hongyan, yellow gingko leaf, Taigi, paper background

Every effort has been made to contact copyright holders of material reproduced in this book. Any omissions will be rectified in subsequent printings if notice is given to the publisher.

All the internet addresses (URLs) given in this book were valid at the time of going to press. However, due to the dynamic nature of the internet, some addresses may have changed, or sites may have changed or ceased to exist since publication. While the author and publisher regret any inconvenience this may cause readers, no responsibility for any such changes can be accepted by either the author or the publisher.

Printed and bound in China.

# CONTENTS

## HUNGRY PREDATORS BEWARE.

Triceratops and other horned dinosaurs may not have had razor-sharp teeth or claws. But many had deadly horns to keep them protected.

These dinosaurs lived between 100 and 65 million years ago, during the Cretaceous Period. Find out more about Triceratops, Centrosaurus, Protoceratops and many other horned dinosaurs.

# ANCHICERATOPS

**PRONOUNCED:** ANG-ki-SER-ah-tops

**NAME MEANING:** near horned face

**TIME PERIOD LIVED:** Late Cretaceous Period, about 72 million years ago

**PHYSICAL FEATURES:** two long horns on its forehead, one short horn on its nose, narrow frill around its neck

**LENGTH:** up to 6 metres (20 feet)

**WEIGHT:** 2.5 metric tons (2.75 tons)

**TYPE OF EATER:** herbivore

Paleontologist Barnum Brown discovered Anchiceratops in 1912. Brown also discovered Tyrannosaurus rex.

Anchiceratops made its home in North America, near today's Wyoming, USA and Alberta, Canada.

N
W E
S

where this
dinosaur lived

Males had shorter
snouts than females.

**ANCHICERATOPS** used its sharp
beak to cut through tough plants
such as conifers and ferns.

5

# ARCHAEOCERATOPS

**PRONOUNCED:** AR-kee-oh-SAIR-a-tops

**NAME MEANING:** ancient horned face

**TIME PERIOD LIVED:** Early Cretaceous Period, about 99 million years ago

**PHYSICAL FEATURES:** large head with a small frill, no horns

**LENGTH:** 0.9 metres (3 feet)

**WEIGHT:** 4.5 kilograms (10 pounds)

**TYPE OF EATER:** herbivore

**ARCHAEOCERATOPS** was one of the smallest dinosaurs in this group.

**ARCHAEOCERATOPS** was discovered in 1992.

Archaeoceratops lived in what is now the north central part of China.

where this dinosaur lived

**ARCHAEOCERATOPS** could stand on its two back legs to run away from predators.

# CENTROSAURUS

**PRONOUNCED:** SEN-tro-SAWR-us

**NAME MEANING:** pointed lizard

**TIME PERIOD LIVED:** Late Cretaceous Period, about 67 million years ago

**PHYSICAL FEATURES:** large horned dinosaur with hooked spikes on its frill

**LENGTH:** 6 metres (20 feet)

**WEIGHT:** 2.7 metric tons (3 tons)

**TYPE OF EATER:** herbivore

Centrosaurus lived in what is now Alberta, Canada.

N
W  E
S

■ **where this dinosaur lived**

**CENTROSAURUS** had rows of sharp teeth to eat plants.

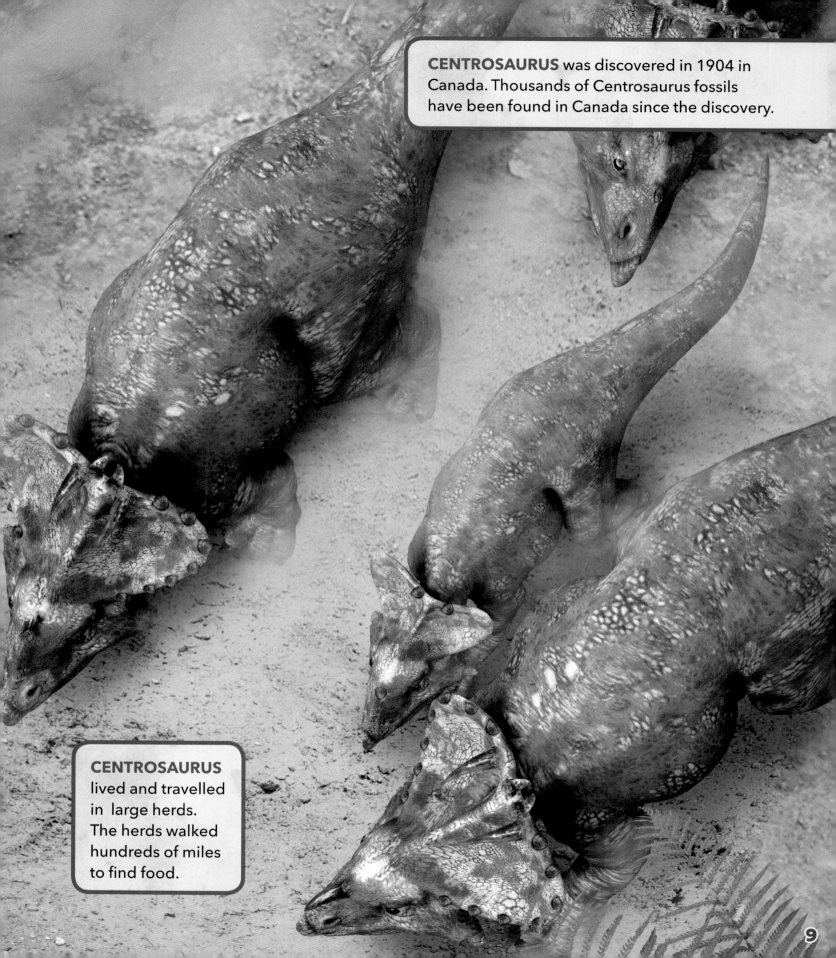

**CENTROSAURUS** was discovered in 1904 in Canada. Thousands of Centrosaurus fossils have been found in Canada since the discovery.

**CENTROSAURUS** lived and travelled in large herds. The herds walked hundreds of miles to find food.

# GRACILICERATOPS

**PRONOUNCED:** GRAS-i-li-SAIR-ah-tops

**NAME MEANING:** graceful horned face

**TIME PERIOD LIVED:** Late Cretaceous Period, about 84 million years ago

**PHYSICAL FEATURES:** sharp beak, bony frill, no horns

**LENGTH:** 0.8 metres (2.6 feet)

**WEIGHT:** 2 kilograms (4.4 pounds)

**TYPE OF EATER:** herbivore

**GRACILICERATOPS** was about the size of a chicken.

**GRACILICERATOPS** could run on its two back legs to escape predators.

Paleontologists first thought **GRACILICERATOPS** was a Microceratus, another dinosaur that lived in Asia. Paleontologists later discovered it was a different dinosaur.

Graciliceratops lived in the Gobi Desert in Asia.

N
W  E
S

where this dinosaur lived

# LEPTOCERATOPS

**PRONOUNCED:** LEP-toh-SER-ah-tops

**NAME MEANING:** little horned face

**TIME PERIOD LIVED:** Late Cretaceous Period, about 66 million years ago

**PHYSICAL FEATURES:** small body, large head

**LENGTH:** 2 metres (6.6 feet)

**WEIGHT:** 68 to 200 kilograms (150 to 441 pounds)

**TYPE OF EATER:** herbivore

**LEPTOCERATOPS** is in the dinosaur group Leptoceratopsidae. Other dinosaurs in this group include Cerasinops and Prenoceratops.

**LEPTOCERATOPS** was about the size of a sheep.

Leptoceratops lived in the plains and forests of what is now western North America.

N
W ← → E
S

where this dinosaur lived

**LEPTOCERATOPS** lived in the same time and place as Triceratops.

# MONTANOCERATOPS

**PRONOUNCED:** mon-TAN-oh-SER-ah-tops

**NAME MEANING:** Montana horned face

**TIME PERIOD LIVED:** Late Cretaceous Period, about 70 million years ago

**PHYSICAL FEATURES:** frill but no horns, narrow tail

**LENGTH:** 3 metres (9.8 feet)

**WEIGHT:** 200 kilograms (440 pounds)

**TYPE OF EATER:** herbivore

The first **MONTANOCERATOPS** fossils were found in 1916.

Unlike other horned dinosaurs, **MONTANOCERATOPS** had claws instead of hooves.

Montanoceratops lived in what is now Montana, USA and Alberta, Canada.

■ where this dinosaur lived

**MONTANOCERATOPS** probably travelled in herds.

Paleontologists originally thought **MONTANOCERATOPS** had a nose horn. Now we know this bone was part of the dinosaur's cheek.

# NEDOCERATOPS

**PRONOUNCED:** ned-oh-SER-a-tops

**NAME MEANING:** insufficient horned face

**TIME PERIOD LIVED:** Late Cretaceous Period, about 70 million years ago

**PHYSICAL FEATURES:** bony frill on the back of its head, two large horns

**LENGTH:** 7 metres (23 feet)

**WEIGHT:** 6 metric tons (6.6 tons)

**TYPE OF EATER:** herbivore

Only one **NEDOCERATOPS** skull has been found.

Nedoceratops lived in the woodlands
of what is now Wyoming, USA.

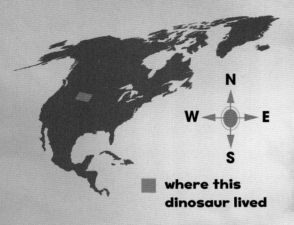

N
W    E
S

■ **where this
dinosaur lived**

**NEDOCERATOPS** was originally
named Diceratops. But an
insect was named Diceratops
first. The dinosaur's name was
changed in 2007.

**NEDOCERATOPS** may be the closest relative to Triceratops.
The dinosaurs looked similar, but Nedoceratops had a shorter
nose and straighter horns over its eyes.

# PACHYRHINOSAURUS

**PRONOUNCED:** pak-i-RIE-no-SAWR-us

**NAME MEANING:** thick-nosed lizard

**TIME PERIOD LIVED:** Late Cretaceous Period, about 70 million years ago

**PHYSICAL FEATURES:** two big horns on its frill, one big lump of bone on its nose

**LENGTH:** 8 metres (26 feet)

**WEIGHT:** 4 metric tons (4.4 tons)

**TYPE OF EATER:** herbivore

**PACHYRHINOSAURUS** had a huge skull for the size of its body.

The first **PACHYRHINOSAURUS** fossils were found in 1946.

**PACHYRHINOSAURUS** rammed into other animals with its bony nose. Males may have pushed each other to show who was the strongest.

Pachyrhinosaurus lived in western North America, in today's Alaska, USA and Alberta, Canada.

N
W · E
S

■ where this dinosaur lived

# PROTOCERATOPS

**PRONOUNCED:** PROH-toh-SER-a-tops

**NAME MEANING:** first horned face

**TIME PERIOD LIVED:** Late Cretaceous Period, about 70 million years ago

**PHYSICAL FEATURES:** no horns, large skull with a tall frill and sharp beak

**LENGTH:** 1.8 metres (6 feet)

**WEIGHT:** 181 kilograms (400 pounds)

**TYPE OF EATER:** herbivore

A **PROTOCERATOPS** nest with 15 eggs inside was discovered in 2011.

Fossils of a **PROTOCERATOPS** and a Velociraptor attacking each other were discovered. Scientists believe both dinosaurs died in the middle of the fight, when a sandstorm blew over them.

Protoceratops lived in the sandy deserts of northern Asia.

where this dinosaur lived

N
W
E
S

Similar to Leptoceratops, **PROTOCERATOPS** was about the size of a sheep.

# STYRACOSAURUS

**PRONOUNCED:** stie-RAK-o-SAWR-us

**NAME MEANING:** spiked lizard

**TIME PERIOD LIVED:** Cretaceous Period, about 75 million years ago

**LENGTH:** 5.5 metres (18 feet)

**WEIGHT:** 3 metric tons (3.3 tons)

**TYPE OF EATER:** herbivore

**PHYSICAL FEATURES:** large horn on its nose, four to six horns around the edge of its frill

**STYRACOSAURUS** has been featured in many films and TV shows.

Styracosaurus lived in what is now Alberta, Canada.

**STYRACOSAURUS** may have used its large frill to knock down trees.

where this dinosaur lived

**STYRACOSAURUS'** nose horn grew up to 56 centimetres (22 inches) long.

# TOROSAURUS

**PRONOUNCED:** TOR-oh-SAWR-us

**NAME MEANING:** pierced lizard

**TIME PERIOD LIVED:** Late Cretaceous Period, about 66 million years ago

**PHYSICAL FEATURES:** large head, long frill, two horns above its eyes and one horn on its nose

**LENGTH:** 9 metres (30 feet)

**WEIGHT:** 4 to 6 metric tons (4.4 to 6.6 tons)

**TYPE OF EATER:** herbivore

TOROSAURUS was a deadly fighter. Its large size and long horns kept predators away.

**TOROSAURUS** was one of the last dinosaurs to die out.

Torosaurus lived in western North America. Fossils have been found from Canada to Texas, USA.

N
W E
S

where this dinosaur lived

Some paleontologists believe **TOROSAURUS** and Triceratops are the same type of dinosaur. But Torosaurus had a shorter nose horn and a longer, flatter frill.

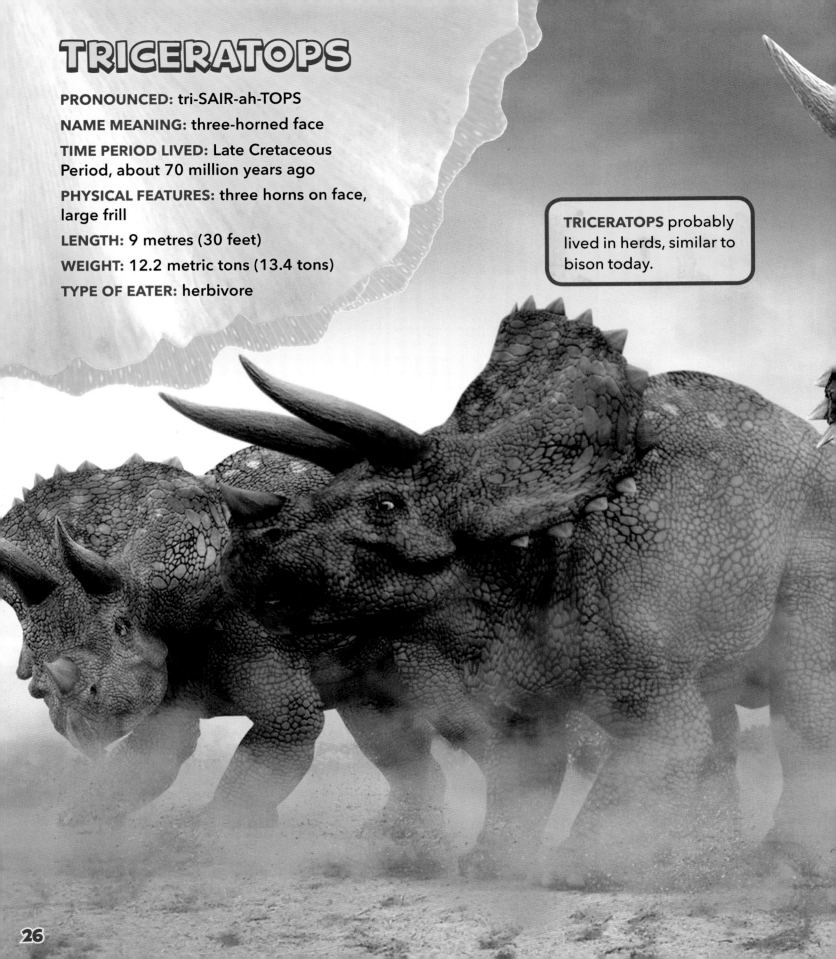

# TRICERATOPS

**PRONOUNCED:** tri-SAIR-ah-TOPS

**NAME MEANING:** three-horned face

**TIME PERIOD LIVED:** Late Cretaceous Period, about 70 million years ago

**PHYSICAL FEATURES:** three horns on face, large frill

**LENGTH:** 9 metres (30 feet)

**WEIGHT:** 12.2 metric tons (13.4 tons)

**TYPE OF EATER:** herbivore

**TRICERATOPS** probably lived in herds, similar to bison today.

**TRICERATOPS** fossils were discovered in 1887. Paleontologists first thought the horns belonged to an ancient bison.

Triceratops lived in North America.

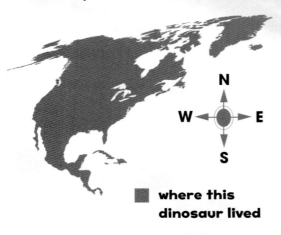

N
W · E
S

**where this dinosaur lived**

**TRICERATOPS** babies had bumps on their faces instead of horns. The bumps grew into horns as the dinosaurs grew older.

**TRICERATOPS** was one of the largest horned dinosaurs.

**TRICERATOPS** used its horns and frill to defend itself from predators such as Tyrannosaurus rex.

Some **TRICERATOPS** skeletons have holes where Tyrannosaurus rex chomped on the bones.

# GLOSSARY

**BEAK** hard, pointed part of an animal's mouth

**BISON** buffalo, an ox-like animal native to North America and Europe

**CONIFER** tree with cones and narrow leaves called needles

**CRETACEOUS PERIOD** third period of the Mesozoic Era; the Cretaceous Period was from 145 to 65 million years ago

**FERN** plant with feathery leaves and no flowers; ferns usually grow in damp places

**FOSSIL** remains of an animal or plant from millions of years ago that have turned to rock

**FRILL** bony collar that fans out around an animal's neck

**HERBIVORE** animal that eats only plants

**HERD** group of the same kind of animals that live and travel together

**PALEONTOLOGIST** scientist who studies fossils

**PREDATOR** animal that hunts other animals for food

**PRONOUNCE** say a word in a certain way

**SANDSTORM** wind storm that blows sand around

**SNOUT** long front part of an animal's head; the snout includes the nose, mouth and jaws

**SPIKE** sharp, pointy object; many dinosaurs used bony spikes to defend themselves

# COMPREHENSION QUESTIONS

**1.** Dinosaurs in this group were herbivores. What is a herbivore?

**2.** How did small dinosaurs in this group such as Archaeoceratops and Graciliceratops keep away from predators?

**3.** Triceratops lived in herds. Name an animal alive today that lives in a herd.

# READ MORE

*Dinosaurs* (First Facts), Charlie Gardner (DK Publishing, 2012)

*Triceratops* (All About Dinosaurs), Daniel Nunn (Raintree 2015)

*Triceratops and other Horned Herbivores* (Dinosaurs!), David West (Franklin Watts, 2015)

# WEBSITES

**www.nhm.ac.uk/discover/dino-directory/index.html**

At this Natural History Museum website you can learn more about dinosaurs through sorting them by name, country and even body shape!

**www.show.me.uk/section/dinosaurs**

This website has loads of fun things to do and see, including a dinosaur mask you can download and print, videos, games, and Top Ten lists.

# INDEX